LOOKING

Observations on

Tan Acharn Kor
Khao-suan-luang

BUDDHIST PUBLICATION SOCIETY
KANDY   **SRI LANKA**

Published in 1991

Buddhist Publication Society
P.O. Box 61
54, Sangharaja Mawatha
Kandy, Sri Lanka

ISBN 955-24-0084-8

Typeset at the BPS using an Atari 1040ST computer and Signum 2.0 software.
Text set in Antikro.

Printed in Sri Lanka by
Karunaratne & Sons Ltd.
647, Kularatne Mawatha
Colombo 10.

THE WHEEL PUBLICATION NO. 373/374

Contents

Introduction

Kor Khao-suan-luang is the penname of Upāsikā Kee Nanayon (1901–1978), one of the foremost women teachers of Dhamma in modern Thailand. Following Thai tradition, she took her penname from the name of the place where she lived: the forested hill in Rajburi where she had established a women's center for practising Dhamma. Although she did not allow men to reside in her center, both men and women were welcome to visit on the weekly Observance days and listen to her talks. Known for the simplicity of her way of life, and for the direct, uncompromising style of her teaching, she had a way with words evident not only in her talks but also in her poetry, which was widely published.

Many of her talks were transcribed and printed for free distribution. Six have already been translated into English and published in a volume entitled *Directing to Self-Penetration* (BPS Wheel No. 326/328). This present collection consists of a brief outline of the practice which she wrote as an introduction to one of her early books of talks, plus excerpts from her later talks which help flesh out the outline.

Although this collection is too brief to serve as a complete guide to the practice, my hope is that it will provide insight and inspiration for all those who, in their search for freedom and happiness, have begun looking inward to the subtleties of their own minds.

The Translator

The Practice in Brief

Those who practise the Dhamma should train themselves to understand in line with the following stages:

The training which is easy to learn, gives immediate results and is suitable for every time, every place, for people of every age and either sex, is to study in *the school of this body*—a fathom long, a cubit wide and a span thick—with its perceiving mind in charge. This body has many things, ranging from the crude to the subtle, which are well worth knowing.

The steps of the training:

1. To begin with, know that the body is composed of various physical properties, the major ones being the properties of earth, water, fire and wind; the minor ones being the aspects which adhere to the major ones, things like colour, smell, shape, etc.

These properties are unstable (inconstant), stressful and full of filth. If you look into them deeply, you will see that there is no substance to them at all. They are simply impersonal conditions, with nothing worth calling "me" or "mine." When you can clearly perceive the body in these terms, you will be able to let go of any clinging or attachment to it as an entity, your self, someone else, this or that.

2. The second step is to deal with mental phenom-

ena (feelings, perceptions, thought-formations and consciousness). Focus on keeping track of the truth that these are characterized by arising, persisting and then disbanding. In other words, their nature is to arise and disband, arise and disband, repeatedly. When you investigate to see this truth, you will be able to let go of your attachments to mental phenomena as entities, as your self, someone else, this or that.

3. Training on the level of practice doesn't simply mean studying, listening or reading. You have to practise so as to see clearly with your own mind in the following steps:

(a) Start out by brushing aside all external concerns and turn to look inside at your own mind until you can know in what ways it is clear or murky, calm or unsettled. The way to do this is to have mindfulness and self-awareness in charge as you keep aware of the body and mind, until you have trained the mind to stay firmly in a state of normalcy.

(b) Once the mind can stay in a state of normalcy, you will see mental formations or preoccupations in their natural state of arising and disbanding. The mind will be empty, neutral and still—neither pleased nor displeased—and will see physical and mental phenomena as they arise and disband naturally, of their own accord.

(c) When the knowledge that there is no self to any of these things becomes thoroughly clear, you will meet with something that lies further inside, beyond all suffering and stress, free from the cycles of change—deathless—free from birth as well as death, since all things that take birth must by nature age, grow ill and die.

(d) When you see this truth clearly, the mind will be empty, not holding onto anything. It won't even assume itself to be a mind or anything at all; it won't latch onto itself as being anything of any sort. All that remains is a pure condition of Dhamma.

(e) Those who see this pure condition of Dhamma in full clarity are bound to grow disenchanted with the repeated sufferings of life. When they know the truth of the world and the Dhamma throughout, they will see the results clearly, right in the present, that *there exists that which lies beyond all suffering*. They will know this without having to ask or take it on faith from anyone, for the Dhamma is *paccattaṁ*, something really to be known for oneself. Those who have seen this truth within themselves will attest to it always.

March 17, 1954

An Hour's Meditation

For those of you who have never sat in meditation, here is how it's done: Fold your legs, one on top of the other, but don't cut off the nerves or the blood flow, or else the breath energy in your legs will stagnate and cause you pain. Sit straight and place your hands one on top of the other on your lap. Hold your head up straight and keep your back straight, too—as if you had a yardstick sticking down your spine. You have to work at keeping it straight, you know. Don't spend the time slouching down and then stretching up again, or else the mind won't be able to settle down and be still....

Keep the body straight and your mindfulness firm—firmly with the breath. However coarse or refined your breath may be, simply breathe in naturally. You don't have to force the breath or tense your body. Simply breathe in and out in a relaxed way. Only then will the mind begin to settle down. As soon as the breath grows normally refined and the mind has begun to settle down, focus your attention on the mind itself. If it slips off elsewhere or any thoughts come in to intrude, simply know right there at the mind. Know the mind right at the mind with every in-and-out breath for the entire hour....

4

When you focus on the breath, using the breath as a leash to tie the mind in place so that it doesn't go wandering off, you have to use your endurance. That is, you have to endure pain. For example, when you sit for a long time there's going to be pain, because you've never sat for so long before. So first make sure that you keep the mind normal and neutral. When pain arises, don't focus on the pain. Let go of it as much as you can. Let go of it and focus on your mind.... For those of you who have never done this before, it may take a while. Whenever any pain or anything arises, if the mind is affected by craving or defilement, it'll struggle because it doesn't want the pain. All it wants is pleasure.

This is where you have to be patient and endure the pain, *because pain is something that has to occur.* If there's pleasure, don't get enthralled with it. If there's pain, don't push it away. Start out by keeping the mind neutral as your basic stance. Then whenever pleasure or pain arises, don't get pleased or upset. Keep the mind continuously neutral and figure out how to let go. If there's a lot of pain, you first have to endure it and then relax your attachments. Don't think of the pain as being *your* pain. Let it be the pain of the body, the pain of nature.

If the mind latches tightly on to anything, it really suffers. It struggles. So here we patiently endure and let go. You have to practise so that you're really good at handling pain. If you can let go of physical pain, you'll be able to let go of all sorts of other suffering and pain as well.... Keep watching the pain, knowing the pain, letting it go. Once you can let it go, you don't have to use a lot of endurance. It takes a lot of endurance only at the beginning. Once the pain arises, separate the mind from it. Let it be the pain of the body. Don't let the mind be pained, too....

This is something that requires equanimity. If you can maintain equanimity in the face of pleasure or pain, it can make the mind peaceful—peaceful even though the pain is still pain. The mind keeps knowing, enduring the pain so as to let it go.

After you've worked at this a good while, you'll come to see how important the ways of the mind are. The mind may be hard to train, but if you keep training it—if you have the time, you can practise at home, at night or early in the morning, keeping watch on your own mind—you'll gain the understanding which comes from mindfulness and discernment. Those who don't train the mind like this go through life—birth, ageing, illness and death—not knowing anything at all about the mind.

When you know your own mind, then when any really heavy illness comes along, the fact that you know your mind will make the pain less and less. But this is something you have to work at doing correctly. It's not easy, yet once the mind is well trained, there's no match for it. It can do away with pain and suffering, and doesn't get restless and agitated. It grows still and cool—refreshed and blooming right there within itself. So try to experience this still, quiet mind....

This is a really important skill to develop, because it will make craving, defilement and attachment grow weaker and weaker. All of us have defilements, you know. Greed, anger and delusion cloud all of our hearts. If we haven't trained ourselves in meditation, our hearts are constantly burning with suffering and stress. Even the pleasure we feel over external things is pleasure only in half-measures, because there's suffering and stress in the delusion that thinks it's pleasure.

As for the pleasure that comes from the practice, it's a cool pleasure tht lets go of everything, really free from any sense of me or mine. I ask that you reach the Dhamma which is the real meat inside this thing which is undisturbed by defilement, undisturbed by pain or anything else.

Even though there's pain in the body, you have to figure out how to let it go. The body is simply the four elements—earth, water, wind and fire. It has to keep showing its inconstancy and stressfulness, so keep your mindfulness neutral, at equanimity. Let the mind be above its feelings—above pleasure, above pain, above everything....

All it really takes is endurance—endurance and relinquishment, letting things go, seeing that they're not us, not ours. This is a point you have to hammer at, over and over again.

When we say you have to endure, you *really* have to endure. Don't be willing to surrender. Craving is going to keep coming up and whispering—telling you to change things, to try for this or that kind of pleasure —but don't you listen to it. You have to listen to the Buddha—the Buddha who tells you to let go of craving. Otherwise craving will plaster and paint things over; the mind will struggle and won't be able to settle down. So you have to give it your all. Look at this hour as a special hour—special in that you're using special endurance *to keep watch on your own heart and mind.*

March 3, 1977

A Basic Order in Life

The most important thing in the daily life of a person who practises the Dhamma is to keep to the precepts and to care for them more than you care for your life—to maintain them in a way that the Noble Ones would praise. If you don't have this sort of regard for the precepts, then the vices which run counter to them will become your everyday habits....

Meditators who think that the breaking of a precept is something trifling and insignificant spoil their entire practice. If you can't practise even these basic, beginning levels of the Dhamma, it will ruin all the qualities you'll be trying to develop in the later stages of the practice. This is why you have to stick to the precepts as your basic foundation, and to keep a lookout for anything in your behavior which falls short of them. Only then will you be able to benefit from your practice for the sake of eliminating your sufferings with greater and greater precision.

If you simply act in line with the cravings and desires which come swelling out of that sense of self which has no fear of the fires of defilement, you'll have to suffer both in this life and in lives to come. If you don't have a sense of conscience—a sense of shame at the thought of doing shoddy actions, and a fear of their consequences—your practice can only deteriorate day by day....

When people live without any order to their lives—without even the basic order that comes with the precepts—there's no way they can attain purity. We have to examine ourselves: In what ways at present are we breaking our precepts in thought, word or deed? If we simply let things pass, if we aren't intent on examining ourselves to see the harm which comes from breaking the precepts and following the defilements, our practice can only sink lower and lower. Instead of extinguishing defilements and suffering, it will simply succumb to the power of craving. If this is the case, what damage is done? How much freedom does the mind lose? These are things we have to learn for ourselves. When we do, our practice of self-inspection in higher matters will get solid results, and won't go straying off into nonsense. For this reason, whenever craving or defilement shows itself in any way in any of our actions, we have to catch hold of it and examine what's going on inside the mind.

Once we are aware with real mindfulness and discernment, we'll see the poison and power of the defilements. We'll feel disgust for them and want to extinguish them as much as we can. But if we use our defilements to examine things, they'll say everything is fine. It's the same as when we're predisposed to liking a certain person: even if that person acts badly, we say he's good. If he acts wrongly, we say he's right. This is the way the defilements are. They say that everything we do is right and throw all the blame on other people, other things. So we can't trust it—

this sense of "self" in which craving and defilement lord it over the heart. We can't trust it at all....

The violence of defilement, or this sense of self, is like that of a fire burning a forest or burning a house: It won't listen to anyone, but simply keeps burning away, burning away inside you. And that's not all. It's always out to set fire to other people, too.

The fires of suffering, the fires of defilement, consume all those who don't contemplate themselves, or who don't have any means of practice for putting them out. People of this sort can't withstand the power of the defilements, can't help but follow along wherever their cravings lead them. The moment they're provoked, they follow in line with these things. This is why the sensations in the mind when it's provoked by defilement are very important, for they can lead you to do things with no sense of shame, no fear for the consequences of doing evil at all—which means that you're sure to break your precepts.

Once you've followed the defilements, they feel really satisfied—like arsonists who feel gleeful when they've set other people's places on fire. As soon as you've called somebody something vile or spread some malicious gossip, the defilements really like it. Your sense of self really likes it, because acting in line with defilement like that gives it real satisfaction. As a consequence, it keeps filling itself with the vices that run counter to the precepts, falling into hell in this very lifetime without realizing it. So take a good look at the violence the defilements do to you, to see whether you should keep socializing with them, to see whether you should regard them as your friends or your enemies....

As soon as any wrong views or ideas come out of the mind, we have to analyze them and turn them around so as to catch sight of the facts within us. No matter what issues the defilements raise, focusing on the faults of others, we have to turn around and look within. *When we realize our own faults and can come to our senses*—that's where our study of the Dhamma, our practice of the Dhamma shows its real rewards.

January 29, 1964

Continuous Practice

The passage for reflection on the four requisites (clothing, food, shelter and medicine) is a fine pattern for contemplation, but we never actually get down to putting it to use. We're taught to memorize it in the beginning, not simply to pass the time of day or so that we can talk about it every now and then, but so that we can use it to contemplate the requisites until we really know them with our own mindfulness and discernment. If we actually get down to contemplating in line with the established pattern, our minds will become much less influenced by unwise thoughts. But it's the rare person who genuinely makes this a continuous practice.... For the most part we're not interested. We don't feel like contemplating this sort of thing. We'd much rather contemplate whether this or that food will taste good or not, and if it doesn't taste good, how to fix it so that it will. That's the sort of thing we like to contemplate.

Try to see the filthiness of food and of the physical properties in general, to see their emptiness of any real entity or self, to see that there is nothing of any substance to the physical properties of the body, which are all rotten and decomposing. The body is like a restroom over a cesspool. We can decorate it on the outside to make it pretty and attractive, but on the inside it's full of the most horrible filthy things. Whenever we excrete anything we ourselves are repelled by it, yet even though we're repelled by it, it's there inside us, in our intestines—decomposing, full of worms, awful smelling. There's just the flimsiest membrane covering it up, but we fall for it and hold tight to it. We don't see the constant decomposition of this body, in spite of the filth and smells it sends out....

The reason we're taught to memorize the passage for reflecting on the requisites, and to use it in our contemplation, is so that we'll see the inconstancy of the body, that there's no "self" to any of it or to any of the mental phenomena we sense at every moment.

* * * * *

We contemplate mental phenomena to see clearly that they're not-self, to see this with every moment. The moments of the mind—the arising, persisting and disbanding of mental sensations—are very subtle and fast. To see them, the mind has to be quiet. If the mind is involved in distractions, thoughts and imaginings, we won't be able to penetrate in to see its characteristics as it deals with its objects, to see what the arising and disbanding within it is like.

This is why we have to practise concentration: to make the mind quiet, to provide a foundation for our contemplation. For instance, you can focus on the breath, or be aware of the mind as it focuses on the breath. Actually, when you focus on the breath, you're also aware of the mind. And again, the mind is what knows the breath. So you focus exclusively on the breath together with the mind. Don't think of anything else, and the mind will settle down and grow still. Once it attains stillness on this level, you've got your chance to contemplate.

Making the mind still so that you can contemplate it is something you have to keep working at in the beginning. The same holds true with training yourself to be mindful and fully aware in all your activities. This is something you really have to work at continuously in this stage, something you have to do all the time. At the same time, you have to arrange the external conditions of your life so that you won't have any concerns to distract you....

Now, of course, the practice is something you can do in any set of circumstances—for example, when you come home from work you can sit and meditate for a while—but when you're trying seriously to make it continuous, to make it habitual, it's much more difficult than that. "Making it habitual" means being fully mindful and aware with each in-and-out breath, wherever you go, whatever you do, whether you're healthy, sick or whatever, and regardless of what happens inside or out. *The mind has to be in a state of all-encompassing awareness while keeping track of the arising and disbanding of mental phenomena at all times*—to the point where you can stop the mind from forming thoughts under the power of craving and defilement the way it used to before you began the practice.

January 14, 1964

Every In-and-Out Breath

Try keeping your awareness with the breath to see what the still mind is like. It's very simple, all the rules have been laid out, but when you actually try to do it, something resists. It's hard. But when you let your mind think 108 or 1009 things, no matter what, it's all easy. It's not hard at all. *Try to see if you can engage your mind with the breath in the same way it's been engaged with the defilements.* Try engaging it with the breath and see what happens. See if you can disperse the defilements with every in-and-out breath. Why is it that the mind can stay engaged with the defilements all day long, and yet go for entire days without knowing how heavy or subtle the breath is at all?

So try to be observant. The bright, clear awareness which stems from staying focused on the mind at all times: sometimes a strong sensory contact comes and can make it blur and fade away with no trouble at all. But if you can keep hold of the breath as a reference point, that state of mind can be more stable and sure, more insured. It has two fences around it. If there's only one fence, it can easily break.

January 29, 1964

Taking a Stance

Normally the mind isn't willing to stop and look, to stop and know itself, which is why we have to keep training it continually so that it will settle down from its restlessness and grow still. Let your desires and thought-processes settle down. Let the mind take its stance in a state of normalcy, not liking or disliking anything. To reach a basic level of emptiness and freedom, you first have to take a stance. If you don't have a stance against which to measure things, progress will be very difficult. If your practice is hit-or-miss—a bit of that, a little of this—you won't get any results. So the mind first has to take a stance.

When you take a stance that the mind can maintain in a state of normalcy, don't go slipping off into the future. Have the mind know itself in the stance of the present: "Right now it's in a state of normalcy. No likes or dislikes have arisen yet. It hasn't created any issues. It's not being disturbed by a desire for this or that."

Then look on in to the basic level of the mind to see if it's as normal and empty as it should be. If you're really looking inside, really aware inside, then *that which is looking and knowing is mindfulness and discernment in and of itself.* You don't need to search for anything anywhere else to come and do your looking for you. As soon as you stop to look, stop to know whether or not the mind is in a state of normalcy, then if it's normal, you'll know immediately that it's normal. If it's not, you'll know immediately that it's not.

Take care to keep this awareness going. If you can keep knowing like this continuously, the mind will be able to keep its stance continuously as well. As soon as the thought occurs to you to check things out, you'll immediately stop to look, stop to know, without any need to go searching for knowledge from anywhere else. You look, you know, right there at the mind, and can tell whether or not it's empty and still. Once you see that it is, then you investigate to see *how* it's empty, *how* it's still. It's not the case that once it's empty, that's the end of the matter; once it's still that's the end of the matter. *That's not the case at all*. You have to keep watch of things, to investigate at all times. Only then will you see the changing—the arising and disbanding—occurring in that emptiness, that stillness, that state of normalcy.

January 14, 1964

The Details of Pain

To lead your daily life by keeping constant supervision over the mind is a way of learning what life is for. It's a way of learning how we can act so as to rid ourselves more and more of suffering and stress— because the suffering and stress caused by defilement, attachment and craving are sure to take all sorts of forms. Only by being aware with true mindfulness and discernment can we comprehend them for what they are. Otherwise we'll simply live obliviously, going wherever events will lead us. This is why mindfulness and discernment are tools for reading yourself, for testing yourself within so that you won't be careless or complacent, oblivious to the fact that suffering is basically what life is all about.

This point is something we really have to comprehend so that we can live without being oblivious. The pains and discontent which fill our bodies and minds all show us the truths of inconstancy, stress and lack of self within us. If you contemplate what's going on inside till you can get down to the details, you'll see the truths appearing within and without, all of which come down to inconstancy, stress and lack of self. But the delusion which is basic to our nature will see everything wrongly—as constant, easeful and self—

and so make us live obliviously, even though there is nothing to guarantee how long our lives will last.

Our dreams and delusions make us forget that we live in the midst of a mass of pain and stress—the stress of defilements, the pain of birth. Birth, ageing, illness and death: All of these are painful and stressful, and lie in the midst of instability and change. They're things we have no control over, for they must circle around in line with the laws of kamma and the defilements we've been amassing all along. Life which floats along in the round of rebirth is thus nothing but stress and pain.

If we can find a way to develop our mindfulness and discernment, they'll be able to cut the round of rebirth so that we won't have to keep wandering on. They'll help us know that birth is painful, ageing is painful, illness is painful, death is painful, and that these are all things which defilement, attachment and craving keep driving through the cycles of change.

So as long as we have the opportunity, we should study the truths which appear throughout our body and mind—and we'll come to know that the elimination of stress and pain, the elimination of defilement, is a function of our practice of the Dhamma. If we don't practise the Dhamma, we'll keep floating along in the round of rebirth which is so drearily repetitious—repetitious in its birth, ageing, illness and death, driven on by defilement, attachment and craving, causing us repeated stress and pain. Living beings for the most part don't know where these stresses and pains come from, or what they come from, because they've never studied them, never contemplated them, so they stay stupid and deluded, wandering on and on without end. ...

If we can stop and be still, the mind will have a chance to be free, to contemplate its sufferings and let them go. This will give it a measure of peace, because it will no longer want anything out of the round of rebirth since it sees that there's nothing lasting to it, that it's simply stress over and over again. Whatever you grab hold of is stress. This is why you need mindfulness and discernment to know and see things for yourself, so that you can supervise the mind and keep it calm, without letting it fall victim to temptation.

This practice is something of the highest importance. People who don't study or practise the Dhamma have wasted their birth as human beings, because they're born deluded and simply stay deluded. But if we study the Dhamma, we'll grow wise to suffering and know the path of practice for freeing ourselves from it. ...

Once we follow the right path, the defilements won't be able to drag us around, won't be able to burn us, because *we're* the ones burning *them* away. We'll come to realize that the more we can burn them away, the more strength of mind we'll gain. If we let the defilements burn us, the mind will be sapped of its strength, which is why this is something you have to be very careful about. Keep trying to burn away the defilements with your every activity, and you'll be storing up strength for your mindfulness and discernment so that they'll be brave in dealing with all sorts of suffering and pain.

You must come to see the world as nothing but stress. There's no real ease to it at all. The awareness we gain from mindfulness and discernment will make us disenchanted with life in the world because it will see things for what they are in every way, both within us and without.

The entire world is nothing but an affair of delusion, an affair of suffering. People who don't know the Dhamma, who don't practise the Dhamma—no matter what their status or position in life—lead deluded, oblivious lives. When they fall ill or are about to die, they're bound to suffer enormously because they haven't taken the time to understand the defilements which burn their hearts and minds in everyday life. Yet if we make a constant practice of studying and contemplating ourselves as our everyday activity, it will help free us from all sorts of suffering and distress. And when this is the case, how can we *not* want to practise?

Only intelligent people, though, will be able to stick with the practice. Foolish people won't want to bother. They would much rather follow the defilements than burn them away. To practise the Dhamma you need a certain basic level of intelligence—enough to have seen at least *something* of the stresses and sufferings that come from defilement. Only then can your practice progress. And no matter how difficult it gets, you'll have to keep practising on to the end.

This practice isn't something you do from time to time, you know. You have to keep at it continuously throughout life. Even if it involves so much physical pain or mental anguish that tears are bathing your cheeks, you have to keep with the chaste life because you're playing for real. If you don't follow the chaste life, you'll get mired in heaps of suffering and flame. So you have to learn your lessons from pain. Try to contemplate it until you can understand it and let it go, and you'll gain one of life's greatest rewards.

Don't think that you were born to gain this or that level of comfort. You were born to study pain and the causes of pain, and to follow the practice that frees you from pain. This is the most important thing there is. Everything else is trivial and unimportant. What's important all lies with the practice.

* * * * *

Don't think that the defilements will go away easily. When they don't come in blatant forms, they come in subtle ones—and the dangers of the subtle ones are hard to see. Your contemplation will have to be subtle too if you want to get rid of them. You'll come to realize that this practice of the Dhamma, in which we contemplate to get to the details inside us, is like sharpening our tools so that when stress and suffering arise we can weaken them and cut them away. If your mindfulness and discernment are brave, the defilements will have to lose out to them. But if you don't train your mindfulness and discernment to be brave, the defilements will crush you to pieces.

We were born to do battle with the defilements and to strengthen our mindfulness and discernment. We'll find that the worth of our practice will grow higher and higher because in our everyday life we've done continuous battle with the stresses and pains caused by defilement, craving and temptation all along—so that the defilements will grow thin and our mindfulness and discernment stronger. We'll sense within ourselves that the mind isn't as troubled and restless as it used to be. It's grown peaceful and calm. The stresses and sufferings of defilement, attachment and craving have grown weaker. Even though we haven't yet wiped them out completely, they've grown continually weaker—because we don't feed them. We don't give them shelter. We do what we can to weaken them so that they grow thinner and thinner each time.

And we have to be brave in contemplating stress and pain, because when we don't feel any great suffering we tend to get complacent. But when the pains and sufferings in our body and mind grow sharp and biting, we have to use our mindfulness and discernment to be strong. *Don't let your spirits be weak*. Only then will you be able to do away with your sufferings and pains.

We have to learn our lessons from pain so that ultimately the mind can gain its freedom from it, instead of being weak and losing out to it all of the time. We have to be brave in doing battle with it to the ultimate extreme until we reach the point where we can let it go.

Pain is something that's always present in this conglomerate of body and mind. It's here for us to see with every moment. If we contemplate it till we know all its details, we can then make it our sport: seeing that the pain is the pain of natural conditions, and not *our* pain. This is something we have to research so as to get to the details: *that it's not our pain*, it's the pain of the *khandhas*. Knowing in this way means that we can separate out the properties—the properties of matter and those of the mind—to see how they interact with one another, how they change. It's something really fascinating.... Watching pain is a way of building up a lot of mindfulness and discernment.

But if you focus on pleasure and ease, you'll simply stay deluded like people in general. They get carried away with the pleasure which comes from watching or listening to the things they like—but then, when pain comes to their bodies and minds to the point where tears are bathing their cheeks, think of how much they suffer! And then they have to be parted from their loved ones, which makes it even worse. But those of us who practise the Dhamma don't need to be deluded like that, because we know and see with every moment that only stress arises, only stress persists, only stress passes away. Aside from stress, nothing arises; aside from stress, nothing passes away. This is there for us to perceive with every moment. If we contemplate it, we'll see it.

So we can't let ourselves be oblivious. This is what the truth is, and we have to study it so as to know it—especially in our life of the practice. We have to contemplate stress all the time to see its every manifestation. The arahants live without being oblivious because they know the truth at all times, and their hearts are clean and pure. As for us with our defilements, we have to keep trying, because if we continually supervise our mind with mindfulness and discernment, we'll be able to keep the defilements from making it dirty and obscured. Even if it does become obscured in any way, we'll be able to remove that obscurity and make the mind empty and free.

This is the practice which weakens all the defilements, attachments and cravings within us. It's because of this practice of the Dhamma that our lives will become free. So I ask you to keep working at the practice without being complacent, because if in whatever span of life is left to you, you keep trying to the full extent of your abilities, you'll gain the mindfulness and discernment to see the facts within yourself, and be able to let go—free from any sense of self, free from any sense of self—continuously.

December 28, 1972

Aware Right at Awareness

The mind, if mindfulness and awareness are watching over it, won't meet with any suffering as the result of its actions. If suffering *does* arise, we'll immediately be aware of it and be able to put it out. This is one point of the practice we can work at constantly. And we can test ourselves by seeing how refined and subtle our all-around awareness is inside the mind. Whenever the mind slips away and goes out to receive external sensory contact: Can it maintain its basic stance of mindfulness or internal awareness? The practice we need to work at in our everyday life is to have constant mindfulness, constant all-around present awareness like this. This is something we work at in every posture: sitting, standing, walking and lying down. Make sure that your mindfulness stays continuous.

Living in this world—the mental and physical phenomena of these five *khandhas*—gives us plenty to contemplate. We must try to watch them, to contemplate them, so that we can understand them—because the truths we must learn to read in this body and mind are here to be read with every moment. We don't have to get wrapped up with any other extraneous themes, because all the themes we need are right here in the body and mind. As long as we can keep the mind constantly aware all round, we can contemplate them.

If you contemplate mental and physical events to see how they arise and disband right in the here and now, and don't get involved with external things— like sights making contact with the eyes, or sounds with the ears—then there really aren't a lot of issues. The mind can be at normalcy, at equilibrium—calm and undisturbed by defilement or the stresses that come from sensory contact. It can look after itself and maintain its balance. You'll come to sense that if you're aware right at awareness in and of itself, without going out to get involved in external things like the mental labels and thoughts that will tend to arise, the mind will see their constant arising and disbanding—and won't be embroiled in anything. This way it can be disengaged, empty and free. But if it goes out to label things as good or evil, as me or mine, or gets attached to anything, it'll become unsettled and disturbed.

You have to know that if the mind can be still, totally and presently aware, and capable of contemplating with every activity, then blatant forms of suffering and stress will dissolve. Even if they start to form, you can be alert to them and disperse them immediately. Once you see this actually happening— even in only the beginning stages—it can disperse a lot of the confusion and turmoil in your heart. In other words, don't let yourself dwell on the past or latch onto thoughts of the future. As for the events arising and passing away in the present, you have to leave them alone. Whatever your duties, simply do them as you have to, and the mind won't get worked up about anything. It will be able, at least to some extent, to be empty and still.

This one thing is something you have to be very careful about. You have to see this for yourself: *that if your mindfulness and discernment are constantly in charge, the truths of the arising and disbanding of mental and physical phenomena are always there for you to see,* always there for you to know. If you look at the body, you'll have to see it simply as physical properties. If you look at feelings, you'll have to see them as changing and inconstant: pleasure, pain, neither pleasure nor pain. To see these things is to see the truth within yourself. Don't let yourself get caught up with your external duties. Simply keep watch in this way inside. If your awareness is the sort that lets you read yourself correctly, the mind will be able to stay at normalcy, at equilibrium, at stillness, without any resistance.

If the mind can stay with itself and not go out looking for things to criticize or latch onto, it can maintain a natural form of stillness. So this is something we have to try for in our every activity. Keep your conversations to a minimum, and there won't be a whole lot of issues. Keep watch right at the mind. When you keep watch at the mind and your mindfulness is continuous, your senses can stay restrained.

Being mindful to keep watch in this way is something you have to work at. Try it and see: Can you keep this sort of awareness continuous? What sort of things can still get the mind engaged? What sorts of thoughts and labels of good and bad, me and mine does it think up? Then look to see if these things arise and disband.

The sensations that arise from external contact and internal contact all have the same sorts of characteristics. You have to look till you can see this. If you know how to look, you'll see it—and the mind will grow calm.

So the point we have to practise in this latter stage doesn't have a whole lot of issues. There's nothing you have to do, nothing you have to label, nothing you have to think a whole lot about. Simply look carefully and contemplate, and in this very lifetime you'll have a chance to be calm and at peace, to know yourself more profoundly within. You'll come to see that the Dhamma is amazing *right here in your own heart*. Don't go searching for the Dhamma outside, for it lies within. Peace lies within, but we have to contemplate so that we're aware all around—subtly, deep down. If you look just on the surface, you won't understand anything. Even if the mind is at normalcy on the ordinary, everyday level, you won't understand much of anything at all.

You have to contemplate so that you're aware all around in a skillful way. The word "skillful" is something you can't explain with words, but you can know for yourself when you see the way in which awareness within the heart becomes special, when you see what this special awareness is about. This is something you can know for yourself.

And there's not really much to it: simply arising, persisting, disbanding. Look until this becomes plain

—really, really plain—and everything disappears. All suppositions, all conventional formulations, all those *khandhas* and properties get swept away, leaving nothing but awareness pure and simple, not involved with anything at all—and there's nothing you have to do to it. Simply stay still and watch, be aware, letting go with every moment.

Simply watching this one thing is enough to do away with all sorts of defilements, all sorts of suffering and stress. If you don't know how to watch it, the mind is sure to get disturbed. It's sure to label things and concoct thoughts. As soon as there's contact at the senses, it'll go looking for things to latch onto, liking and disliking the objects it meets in the present, and then getting involved with the past and future, spinning a web to entangle itself.

If you truly look at each moment in the present, there's really nothing at all. You'll see with every mental moment that things disband, disband, disband—really nothing at all. The important point is that you don't go forming issues out of nothing. The physical elements perform their duties in line with their elementary physical nature. The mental elements keep sensing in line with their own affairs. But our stupidity is what goes looking for issues to cook up, to label, to think about. It goes looking for things to latch onto, and then gets the mind into a turmoil. This point is all we really have to see for ourselves. This is the problem we have to solve for ourselves. If things are left to their nature, pure and simple, there's no "us," no "them." This is a singular truth which will arise for us to know and see. There's nothing else we can know or see that can match it in any way. Once you know and see this one thing, it extinguishes all suffering and stress. The mind will be empty and free, with no meanings, no attachments, for anything at all.

This is why looking inward is so special in so many ways. Whatever arises, simply stop still to look at it. Don't get excited by it. If any special intuitions arise when the mind is still, then if you become excited you'll get the mind worked up into a turmoil. If you become afraid that this or that will happen, that too will get you in a turmoil. So you have to stop and look, stop and know. The first thing is simply to look. The first thing is simply to know. And don't latch onto what you know—because whatever it is, it's simply a phenomenon which arises and disbands, arises and disbands, changing as part of its nature.

So your awareness has to take a firm stance right at the mind in and of itself. In the beginning stages you have to know that when mindfulness is standing firm, the mind won't be affected by the objects of sensory contact. Keep working at maintaining this stance, holding firm to this stance. If you gain a sense of this for yourself, really knowing and seeing for yourself, your mindfulness will become even more firm. If anything arises in any way at all, you'll be able to let it go—and all the many troubles and turmoils of the mind will dissolve away.

If mindfulness slips and the mind goes out giving meanings to anything, latching onto anything, troubles will arise, so you have to keep checking on this with every moment. There's nothing else that's so worth checking on. You have to keep check on the mind in and of itself, contemplating the mind in and of itself. Or else you can contemplate the body in and of itself, feelings in and of themselves, or the phenomena of arising and disbanding—i.e. the Dhamma in and of itself. All of these things are themes you can keep track of entirely within yourself. You don't have to keep track of a lot of themes, because having a lot of themes is what will make you restless and distracted. First you'll practise this theme, then you'll practise that, then you'll make comparisons, all of which will keep the mind from growing still.

If you can take your stance at awareness, if you're skilled at looking, the mind can be at peace. You'll know how things arise and disband. First practise keeping awareness right within yourself so that your mindfulness can be firm, without being affected by the objects of sensory contact, so that it won't label things as good or bad, pleasing or displeasing. You have to keep checking to see that when the mind can be at normalcy, centered and neutral as its primary stance, then—whatever it knows or sees—it will be able to contemplate and let go.

The sensations in the mind that we explain at such length are still on the level of labels. Only when there can be *awareness right at awareness* will you really be able to know that the mind which is aware of awareness in this way doesn't send its knowing outside of this awareness. There are no issues. Nothing can be concocted in the mind when it knows in this way. In other words:

> An inward-staying
> unentangled knowing,
> All outward-going knowing
> cast aside.

The only thing you have to work at maintaining in the mind is this state of normalcy—knowing, seeing and still in the present. If you don't maintain it, if you don't keep looking after it, then when sensory contact comes it will have an effect. The mind will go out with labels of good and bad, liking and disliking. So make sure you maintain the basic awareness which is aware right at yourself. And don't let there be any labeling. No matter what sort of sensory contact comes, you have to make sure that this awareness comes first.

If you train yourself correctly in this way, everything will stop. You won't go straying out through your senses of sight, hearing, etc. The mind will stop and look, stop and be aware right at awareness, so as to know the truth that everything arises and disbands. There's no real truth to anything. Only our stupidity is what latches onto things, giving them meanings and then suffering for it—suffering because of its ignorance, suffering because of its unacquaintance with the five *khandhas*—form, feelings, perceptions, thought-formations and cognizance—all of which are inconstant, stressful and not-self.

Use mindfulness to gather your awareness together, and the mind will stop getting unsettled, stop running after things. It will be able to stop and be still. Then make it know in this way, see in this way *constantly*—at every moment, with every activity. Work at watching and knowing the mind in and of itself: that will be enough to cut away all sorts of issues. You won't have to concern yourself with them at all.

If the body is in pain, simply keep watch of it. You can simply keep watch of feelings in the body because the mind which is aware of itself in this way can keep watch of anything within or without. Or it can simply be aware of itself to the point where it lets go of things outside, lets go of sensory contact and keeps constant watch on the mind in and of itself. That's when you'll know that this is what the mind is like when it's at peace: it doesn't give meanings to anything. This is the emptiness of the mind which is unattached, uninvolved, unconcerned with anything at all.

These words—unattached, uninvolved and unconcerned—are things you have to consider carefully, because what they refer to is subtle and deep. "Uninvolved" means uninvolved with sensory contact, undisturbed by the body or feelings; "unconcerned" means not worried about the past, the future or the present. You have to contemplate these things until you know them skillfully. Even though they're subtle, you have to contemplate them until you know them thoroughly. And don't go concerning yourself with external things, because they'll keep you unsettled, keep you running, keep you distracted with labels and thoughts of good and bad and all that sort of thing. You have to put a stop to these things. If you don't, your practice won't accomplish anything, because these things keep playing up to you and deceiving you. Once you see anything it will fool you into seeing it as right, wrong, good, bad and so forth.

Eventually you have to come down to the awareness that everything simply arises, persists and then disbands. *Make sure you stay focused on the disbanding.* If you watch just the arising, you may get carried off on a tangent, but if you focus on the disbanding you'll see emptiness: everything is disbanding every instant. No matter what you look at, no matter what you see, it's there for just an instant and then disbands. Then it arises again. Then it disbands. There's simply arising, knowing, disbanding.

So let's watch what happens of its own accord— because the arising and disbanding which occurs by way of the senses is something that happens of its own accord. You can't prevent it. You can't force it. If you look and know it without attachment, there will be none of the harm that comes from joy or sorrow. The mind will stay in relative normalcy and neutrality. But if you're forgetful and start latching on, labeling things in pairs in any way at all—good and bad, happy and sad, pleasing and displeasing—the mind will become unsettled: no longer empty, no longer still. When this happens you have to probe on in to know why.

All the worthless issues that arise in the mind have to be cut away. Then you'll find that you have less and less to say, less and less to talk about, less and less to think about. These things grow less and less on their own. They stop on their own. But if you get involved in a lot of issues, the mind won't be able to stay still. *So we have to keep watching things that are completely worthless and without substance*, to see that they're not-self. Keep watching them repeatedly, because your awareness, coupled with the mindfulness and discernment which will know the truth, has to see that "This isn't my self. There's no substance or worth to it at all. It simply arises and disbands right here. It's here for just an instant, and then it disbands."

All we have to do is stop and look, stop and know clearly in this way, and we'll be able to do away with many, many kinds of suffering and stress. The normal stress of the *khandhas* will still occur—we can't prevent it—but we'll know that it's the stress of nature, and won't latch onto it as ours.

So we keep watch of things which happen on their own. If we know how to watch, we keep watching things which happen on their own. Don't latch onto them as being you or yours. Keep this awareness firmly established in itself, as much as you can, and there won't be much else you'll have to remember or think about.

When you keep looking, keep knowing like this at all times, you'll come to see that there are no big issues going on. There's just the issue of arising, persisting and disbanding. You don't have to label anything as good or bad. If you simply look in this way, it's no great weight on the heart. But if you go dragging in issues of good and bad, self and all that, then suffering starts in a big way. The defilements start in a big way, and they weigh on the heart, making it troubled and upset. So you have to stop and look, stop and investigate really deep down inside. It's like water covered with duckweed: only when we take our hand to part the duckweed and take a look will we see that the water beneath it is crystal clear.

As you look into the mind, you have to part it, you have to stop: stop thinking, stop labeling things as good or bad, stop everything. You can't go branding anything. Simply keep looking, keep knowing. When the mind is quiet you'll see that there's nothing there. Everything is all still. Everything has all stopped inside. But as soon as there's labeling, even in the stillness, the stopping, the quiet, it will set things in motion. And as soon as things get set into motion and you don't know how to let go right from the start, issues will arise, waves will arise. Once there are issues and waves, they strike the mind and it goes splashing all out of control. This splashing of the mind includes craving and defilement as well, because *avijjā*—ignorance—lies at its root....

Our major obstacle is this aggregate of perceptions, of labels. If we aren't aware of the arising and disbanding of perceptions, these labels will take hold. Perceptions are the chief instigators which label things within and without, so we have to be aware of their arising and disbanding. Once we're aware in this way, perceptions will no longer function as a cause of suffering; they won't give rise to any further thought-formations. The mind will be aware in itself and able to extinguish these things in itself.

So we have to stop things at the level of perception. If we don't, thought-formations will fashion things into issues and then cause consciousness to wobble and waver in all sorts of ways. But these are things we can stop and look at, things we can know with every mental moment.... If we aren't yet really acquainted with the arising and disbanding in the mind, we won't be able to let go. We can talk about letting go, but we can't do it because we don't yet know. As soon as anything arises we grab hold of it—even when actually it's already disbanded, but since we don't really see, we don't know....

So I ask that you understand this basic principle. Don't go grasping after this thing or that, or else you'll get yourself all unsettled. The basic theme is within: look on in, keep knowing on in until you penetrate everything. The mind will then be free from turmoil. Empty. Quiet. Aware. So keep continuous watch of the mind in and of itself, and you'll come to the point where you simply run out of things to say. Everything will stop on its own, grow still on its own, *because the underlying condition which has stopped and is still is already there,* it's simply that we aren't aware of it yet.

November 3, 1975

The Pure Present

We have to catch sight of the sensation of knowing when the mind gains knowledge of anything and yet isn't aware of itself, to see how it latches onto things—physical form, feeling, perceptions, thought-formations and consciousness. We have to probe on in and look on our own. We can't use the teachings we've memorized to catch sight of these things. That won't get us anywhere at all. We may remember, "The body is inconstant," but even though we can say it, we can't see it.

We have to focus on in to see exactly *how* the body is inconstant, to see how it changes. And we have to focus on feelings—pleasant, painful and neutral—to see how they change. The same holds true with perceptions, thought-formations and so forth: we have to focus on them, investigate them, contemplate them to see their characteristics *as they actually are.*

Even if you can see these things for only a moment, it'll do you a world of good. You'll be able to catch yourself. The things you thought you knew, you didn't really know at all.... This is why the knowledge we gain in the practice has to keep changing through many, many levels. It doesn't stay on just one level.

So even when you're able to know arising and disbanding with every moment right in the present, if your contemplation isn't continuous, it won't be very clear.

You have to know how to contemplate the bare sensation of arising and disbanding, simply arising and disbanding, without any labels of "good" or "bad." Just keep with the pure sensation of arising and disbanding. When you do this, other things will come to intrude—but no matter how they intrude, it's still a matter of arising and disbanding, so you can keep your stance with arising and disbanding in this way.

If you start labeling things, it gets confusing. All you need to do is keep looking at the right spot: the bare sensation of arising and disbanding. Simply make sure that you really keep watch of it. Whether there's awareness of sights, sounds, smells, tastes or tactile sensations, just stay with the sensation of arising and disbanding. Don't go labeling the sight, sound, smell, taste or tactile sensation. If you can keep watch in this way, you're with the pure present—and there won't be any issues.

When you keep watch in this way, you're keeping watch on inconstancy, on change, as it actually occurs—because even the arising and disbanding changes. It's not the same thing arising and disbanding all the time. First this sort of sensation arises and disbands, then that sort arises and disbands. If you keep watch on bare arising and disbanding like this, you're sure to arrive at insight. But if you keep watch with labels—"That's the sound of a cow," "That's the bark of a dog"—you won't be watching the bare sensation of sound, the bare sensation of arising and disbanding. As soon as there's labeling, thought-formations come along with it. Your senses of touch, sight, hearing and so forth will continue their bare arising and disbanding, but you won't know it. Instead, you'll label everything: sights, sounds, etc., and then there will be attachments, feelings of pleasure and displeasure, and you won't know the truth.

The truth keeps going along on its own. Sensations keep arising and then disbanding. If we focus right here—at the consciousness of the bare sensation of sights, sounds, smells, tastes and tactile sensations, we'll be able to gain insight quickly....

If we know how to observe things in this way, we'll easily be able to see when the mind is provoked by passion or greed, and even more easily when it's provoked by anger. As for delusion, that's something more subtle ... something you have to take a great interest in and investigate carefully. You'll come to see all sorts of hidden things—how the mind is covered with many, many layers of film. It's really fascinating. But then that's what insight meditation is for—to open our eyes so that we can know and see, so that we can destroy our delusion and ignorance.

June 3, 1964

The Deceits of Knowing

You have to find approaches for contemplating and probing at all times so as to catch sight of the flickerings of awareness, to see in what ways it streams out to know things. Be careful to catch sight of it both when its knowing is right and when it's wrong. Don't mix things up, taking wrong knowledge for right, or right knowledge for wrong. This is something extremely important for the practice, this question of right and wrong knowing, for these things can play tricks on you.

When you gain any new insights, don't go getting excited. You can't let yourself get excited by them at all, because it doesn't take long for your insight to change—to change right now, before your very eyes. It's not going to change at some other time or place. It's changing right now. You have to know how to observe, how to acquaint yourself with the deceits of knowledge. *Even when it's correct knowledge, you can't latch onto it.*

Even though we may have standards for judging what sort of knowledge is correct in the course of our practice, don't go latching onto correct knowledge—because correct knowledge is inconstant. It changes. It can turn into false knowledge, or into knowledge

43

which is even more correct. You have to contemplate things very carefully, very, very carefully so that you won't fall for your knowledge, thinking, "I've gained right insight; I know better than other people"—so that you won't start assuming yourself to be special. The moment you assume yourself, your knowledge immediately turns wrong. Even if you don't let things show outwardly, the mere mental event in which the mind labels itself is a form of wrong knowing which obscures the mind from itself in an insidious way.

This is why meditators who tend not to contemplate things, who don't catch sight of the deceits of every form of knowledge—right and wrong, good and bad—tend to get bogged down in their knowledge. The knowledge which deceives them into thinking, "What I know is right," gives rise to strong pride and conceit within them, without their even realizing it.

This is because the defilements are always getting into the act without our realizing it. They're insidious, and in their insidious way they keep getting into the act as a matter of course, for the defilements and mental effluents are all still there in our character. Our practice is basically a probing deep inside, from the outer levels of the mind to the inner ones. This is an approach which requires a great deal of subtlety and precision.... *The mind has to use its own mindfulness and discernment to dig everything out of itself, leaving just the mind in and of itself, the body in and of itself, and then keep watch of them.*

* * * * *

The basic challenge in the practice is this one point and nothing else: *this problem of how to look inward so that you see clear through.* If the mind hasn't been trained to look inward, it tends to look outward, simply waiting to receive its objects from outside— and all it gets is the confusion of its sensations going in and out, in and out. And even though this confusion is one aspect of change and inconstancy, we don't see it that way. Instead, we see it as issues, good and bad, pertaining to the self. When this is the case, we're back right where we started, not knowing what's what. This is why the mind's sensations, when it isn't acquainted with itself, are so secretive and hard to perceive. If you want to find out about them by reading a lot of books, you end up piling more defilements onto the mind, making it even more thickly covered than before.

So when you turn to look inward, you shouldn't use concepts and labels to do your looking for you. If you use concepts and labels to do your looking, there will be nothing but concepts arising, changing and disbanding. Everything will get all concocted into thoughts—and then how will you be able to watch in utter silence? The more you take what you've learned from books to look inside yourself, the less you'll see.

So whatever you've learned, when you come to the practice you have to put all the labels and concepts you've gained from your learning to one side. You have to make yourself an innocent beginner once more. Only then will you be able to penetrate in to read the truths within you. If you carry all the para-

phernalia of the concepts and standards you've gained from your learning to gauge things inside you, you
can search to your dying day and yet won't meet with
any real truths at all. This is why you have to hold to
only one theme in your practice. If the mind has lots
of themes to concern itself with, it's still just wandering around—wandering around to know this and
that, going out of bounds without realizing it, and not
really wanting to know itself. This is why those with
a lot of learning like to teach others, to show off
their level of understanding. And this is precisely how
the desire to stand out keeps the mind obscured....

Of all the various kinds of deception, *there's none
as bad as deceiving yourself.* When you haven't yet
really seen the truth, what business do you have making assumptions about yourself, that you've attained
this or that sort of knowledge, or that you know
enough to teach others correctly? The Buddha is
quite critical of teachers of this sort. He calls them
"people in vain." Even if you can teach large numbers
of people to become arahants, while you yourself
haven't tasted the flavour of the Dhamma, the Buddha says that you're a person in vain. So you have to
keep examining yourself. If you haven't yet really
trained yourself in the things you teach to others,
how will you be able to extinguish your own suffering?

Think about this for a moment. Extinguishing suffering, gaining release from suffering: Aren't these
subtle matters? Aren't they completely personal
within us? If you question yourself in this way, you'll
be on the right track. But even then you have to be

careful: if you start taking sides with yourself, the mind will cover itself up with wrong insights and wrong opinions. If you don't observe really carefully, you can get carried away on a tangent—because the awareness with which the mind reads itself and actually sees through itself is something really extraordinary, really worth developing, and it really eliminates suffering and defilement. This is the real, honest truth, not a lot of propaganda or lies. It's something you really have to practise, and then you'll really have to see clearly in this way. When this is the case, how can you *not* want to practise?

If you examine yourself correctly in this way, you'll be able to know what's real. But you have to be careful to examine yourself correctly. If you start latching on to any sense of self, thinking that you're better than other people, you've failed the examination. No matter how correct your knowledge, you have to keep humble and respectful above all else. You can't let there be any pride or conceit at all, or it will destroy everything.

This is why the awareness that eliminates the sense of self depends more than anything else on your powers of observation—to check and see if there's still anything in your knowledge or opinions that comes from the force of pride in any sense of self.... You have to use the full power of your mindfulness and discernment to cut these things away. It's nothing you can play around at. If you gain a few insights or let go of things a bit, don't go thinking you're anything special. The defilements don't hold a truce with anyone. They keep coming right out as they like. So you have to be circumspect and examine things on all sides. Only then will you be able to benefit in ways that make your defilements and sufferings lighter and lighter.

When we probe in to find the instigator—the mind, or this property of consciousness—that's when we're on the right track, and our probing will keep getting results, will keep weakening the germs of craving and wiping them out. In whatever way craving streams out, for "being" or "having" in whatever way at all, we'll be able to catch sight of it every time. To catch hold and examine this "being" and "having" in this way, though, requires a lot of subtlety. If you aren't really mindful and discerning, you won't be able to catch sight of these things at all, because the mind is continually wanting to be and to have. The germs of defilement lie hidden deep in the seed of the mind, in this property of consciousness. Simply to be aware of them skillfully is no mean feat—so we shouldn't even *think* of trying to wipe them out with our mere opinions. We have to keep contemplating, probing on in, until things come together just right, in a single moment, and then it's like reaching the basic level of knowing which exists on its own, with no willing or intention at all.

This is something that requires careful observation: the difference between willed knowing and unwilled knowing. Sometimes there's the intention to look and be aware within, but there come times when there's no intention to look within, and yet knowledge arises on its own. If you don't yet know, look at the intention to look inward: what is it like? What is it looking for? What does it see? This is a basic approach you have to hold to. This is a level you have to work at, and one in which you have to make use of intention—the intention to look inward in this way.... But once you reach the basic level of knowing, then as soon as you happen to focus down and look within, the knowledge will be there on its own.

January 29, 1964

Sabbe Dhammā Anattā

One night I was sitting in meditation outside in the open air—my back straight as an arrow—firmly determined to make the mind quiet, but even after a long time it wouldn't settle down. So I thought, "I've been working at this for many days now, and yet my mind won't settle down at all. It's time to stop being so determined and to simply be aware of the mind." I started to take my hands and feet out of the meditation posture, but at the moment I had unfolded one leg but had yet to unfold the other, I could see that my mind was like a pendulum swinging more and more slowly, more and more slowly—until it stopped.

Then there arose an awareness which was sustained by itself. Slowly I put my legs and hands back into position. At the same time, the mind was in a state of awareness absolutely and solidly still, seeing clearly into the elementary phenomena of existence as they arose and disbanded, changing in line with their nature—and also seeing a separate condition inside, with no arising, disbanding or changing, a condition beyond birth and death: something very difficult to put clearly into words, because it was a realization of the elementary phenomena of nature, completely internal and individual.

After a while I slowly got up and lay down to rest. This state of mind remained as a stillness which sustained itself deep down inside. Eventually the mind came out of this state and gradually returned to normal.

From this I was able to observe how practice consisting of nothing but fierce desire simply upsets the mind and keeps it from being still. But when one's awareness of the mind is just right, an inner awareness will arise naturally of its own accord. Because of this clear inner awareness, I was able to continue knowing the facts of what is true and false, right and wrong, from that point on, and it enabled me to know that the moment when the mind let go of everything was a clear awareness of the elementary phenomena of nature, because it was an awareness that knew within and saw within of its own accord—not something you can know or see by wanting.

For this reason the Buddha's teaching, *"Sabbe dhammā anattā*—All phenomena are not-self," tells us not to latch onto *any* of the phenomena of nature, whether conditioned or conditionless. From that point on I was able to understand things and let go of attachments step by step.

July 9, 1971

Going Out Cold

It's important to realize how to focus on events in order to get special benefits from your practice. *You have to focus so as to observe and contemplate, not simply to make the mind still.* Focus on *how* things arise, *how* they disband. Make your focus subtle and deep.

When you're aware of the characteristics of your sensations, then—if it's a physical sensation—contemplate that physical sensation. There will have to be a feeling of stress. Once there's a feeling of stress, how will you be aware of it simply as a feeling so that it won't lead to anything further? Once you can be aware of it simply as a feeling, it stops right there without producing any taste in terms of a desire for anything. The mind will disengage right there— right there at the feeling. If you don't focus on it in this way, craving will arise on top of the feeling— craving to attain ease and be rid of the stress and pain. If you don't focus on the feeling in the proper way right from the start, craving will arise before you're aware of it, and if you then try to let go of it, it'll be very tiring....

The way in which preoccupations take shape, the sensations of the mind as it's aware of things coming with every moment, the way these things change and disband: these are all things you have to focus on to see clearly.

This is why we disengage the mind. We don't disengage it so that it doesn't know or amount to anything. That's not the kind of disengagement we want. *The more the mind is truly disengaged, the more it sees clearly into the characteristics of the arising and disbanding within itself.*

All I ask is that you observe things carefully, that your awareness be all-around at all times. Work at this as much as you can. If you can keep this sort of awareness going, you will find that the mind or consciousness under the supervision of mindfulness and discernment in this way is different from—is the opposite of—consciousness which is unsupervised. It will be the opposite sort of thing continually.

If you keep the mind well supervised so that it's sensitive in the proper way, it will yield enormous benefits, not just small ones. If you don't make it properly sensitive and aware, what can you expect to gain from it?

When we say that we gain from the practice, we're not talking about anything else. We're talking about gaining disengagement. Freedom. Emptiness. Before, the mind was embroiled. Defilement and craving attacked and robbed it, leaving it completely entangled. Now it's disengaged, freed from the defilements which used to gang up to burn it. Its desires for this or that thing, its concocting of this or that thought, have all fallen away. So now it's empty and disengaged. It can be empty in this way right before your very eyes. Try to see it right now, before your eyes, right now as I'm speaking and you're listening. Probe on in so as to know.

If you can be constantly aware in this way, you're following in the footsteps or taking within you the quality called "*buddho*," which means one who knows, who is awake, who has blossomed in the Dhamma. Even if you haven't fully blossomed—if you've blossomed only to the extent of disengaging from the blatant levels of craving and defilement— you still benefit a great deal, for when the mind really knows the defilements and can let them go, it feels cool and refreshed in and of itself. This is the exact opposite of the defilements which, as soon as they arise, make us burn and smoulder inside. If we don't have the mindfulness and discernment to help us know, the defilements will burn us. But as soon as mindfulness and discernment know, the fires go out—they go out cold.

Observe how the defilements arise and take shape—they also disband as well. They arise and disband, arise and disband in quick succession, but when they disband on their own in this way, go out on their own in this way, they go out hot. If we have mindfulness and discernment watching over them, they go out cold. Look so that you can see what the true knowledge of mindfulness and discernment is like: it goes out; it goes out cold. As for the defilements, even when they arise and disband in line with their nature, they go out hot—hot because we latch onto them, hot because of attachment. When they go out cold, look again—it's because there's no attachment.

They've been let go, put out.

This is something really worth looking into: the fact that there's something very special like this in the mind—*special in that when it really knows the truth, it isn't attached*. It's disengaged, empty and free. This is how it's special. It can grow empty of greed, anger and delusion, step after step. It can be empty of desire, empty of mental processes. The important thing is that you really see for yourself that the true nature of the mind is that it can be empty.... This is why I said this morning that *nibbāna* doesn't lie anywhere else. It lies right here, right where things go out and are cool, go out and are cool. It's staring us right in the face.

May 26, 1964

Reading the Heart

The Buddha taught us to know with our own hearts and minds. Even though there are many, many words and phrases coined to explain the Dhamma, we need focus only on the things we can know and see, extinguish and let go of right in each moment of the immediate present—better than taking on a load of other things. Once we can read and comprehend our inner awareness, we'll be struck deep within us that the Buddha awakened to the truth right here in the heart. His truth is truly the language of the heart.

When they translate the Dhamma in all sorts of ways, it becomes something ordinary. But if you keep close and careful watch right at the heart and mind, you'll be able to see clearly, to let go, to put down your burdens. If you don't know right here, your knowledge will send out all sorts of branches, turning into thought-formations with all sorts of meanings in line with conventional labels—and all of them way off the mark.

If you know right at your inner awareness and make it your constant stance, there's nothing at all: no need to take hold of anything, no need to label anything, no need to give anything names. Right where craving arises, right where it disbands: that's where you'll know what *nibbāna is like.* ...

"*Nibbāna* is simply this disbanding of craving"— that's what the Buddha stressed over and over again.

March 15, 1974

DIRECTING TO SELF-PENETRATION
Acharn Kor Khao-suan-luang

This collection of six Dhamma talks by the remark-able Thai woman meditation teacher Acharn Kor focuses on the theme of "centering the mind in non-attachment." The talks, delivered to her students at her meditation centre, speak with an astounding power of truth which reveals the deep experience of the teacher. *Contents*: Training in Renunciation; Making Dhamma One's True Concern; Establishing a Foundation of Mindfulness; Struggling Against the Defilements' Hordes; The Practice to Overcome Suffering; Training for Liberation.

"When one understands suffering, one strenuously sets one's course straight for the farther shore where all desires and defilements are extinguished. With insight one penetrates to see the common characteristics of impermanence, suffering and not-self in the aggregates. Those with mindfulness and wisdom must concentrate on annihilating the defilements, for should a germ remain it will lead to renewed suffering. Therefore steadily investi-gate and release and eliminate—this is certainly the right way!"

Wheel No. 326/328   80 pages

Price as in our latest catalog